The Daily Norwegian Challenge

Learn 10 Norwegian Words a Day for 7 Weeks

Introduction

🪨 Welcome to "Learn 10 Norwegian Words a Day for 7 Weeks"! Designed to assist kids 🧒 and beginners eager to master the Norwegian language 🚩. With hand-picked words and fun, interactive activities 🎮, we promise an enjoyable learning experience.

✳️ Learning a new language opens up a world of excitement, but it can be a challenge. Don't fret! We've crafted this book with you in mind. Every day, discover 🔍 ten practical Norwegian words for daily scenarios. These cover diverse topics, ensuring a richer vocabulary and boosted confidence in speaking 🗣.

To make learning smoother, we've juxtaposed English 🏴 words alongside Norwegian ones. Engage in writing 👆 the Norwegian equivalents frequently to embed them in memory, setting a solid base. Embrace the daily joy of uncovering new terms, advancing your linguistic prowess step by step.

This guide will accompany you for seven thrilling weeks 📓. Each week introduces fresh words while revisiting previously learned ones. Carve out a little time ⏰ every day for the exercises and challenges. Remember, consistency is key 🔑, and your diligence will bear fruits 🍎.

Whether you're a budding language aficionado or just getting started, this book is tailored for you. Vibrant illustrations 🐦 and engaging tasks ensure you stay hooked. We believe in making language acquisition delightful and aspire to kindle your passion for Norwegian.

As you embark on this linguistic voyage ⛰️, embrace hurdles, celebrate milestones 🎉, and above all, relish the process. Aiming for 10 Norwegian words daily is attainable. Commitment and tenacity will pave the way for enhanced communication and insight 🌐.

Dive in and enjoy learning! 🔥📖

Table of Contents

Week 1

Day 1: Numbers

One	En [ehn]
Two	To [too]
Three	Tre [treh]
Four	Fire [fee-reh]
Five	Fem [fem]
Six	Seks [seks]
Seven	Syv [sev]
Eight	Åtte [AW-teh]
Nine	Ni [nee]
Ten	Ti [tee]

Write the right words down twice on the next page

Six	....	....
Two	....	....
Eight	....	....
Four	....	....
Five	....	....
Eight	....	....
Seven	....	....
Three	....	....
Nine	....	....
Ten	....	....
One	....	....
Two	....	....
Ten	....	....
Four	....	....
Five	....	....
Six	....	....
Seven	....	....
Three	....	....
Nine	....	....
One	....	....

Week 1

Day 2: Colors

Red	Rød [rœd]
Blue	Blå [blaw]
Yellow	Gul [gool]
Green	Grønn [grœn]
Orange	Oransje [o-RAN-she]
Purple	Lilla [LIL-lah]
Pink	Rosa [RO-sah]
Black	Svart [svart]
White	Hvit [kvit]
Gray	Grå [graw]

Write the right words down twice on the next page

Red	....	....
Purple	....	....
White	....	....
Gray	....	....
Orange	....	....
Purple	....	....
Blue	....	....
Black	....	....
White	....	....
Gray	....	....
Pink	....	....
Blue	....	....
Yellow	....	....
Green	....	....
Orange	....	....
Pink	....	....
Red	....	....
Black	....	....
Yellow	....	....
Green	....	....

Week 1

Day 3: Family

Mother	Mor [moor]
Father	Far [far]
Brother	Bror [broor]
Sister	Søster [SUHS-ter]
Son	Sønn [sœn]
Daughter	Datter [dat-ter]
Grandfather	Bestefar [BES-teh-far]
Grandmother	Bestemor [BES-teh-moor]
Uncle	Onkel [ONG-kel]
Aunt	Tante [TAN-teh]

Write the right words down twice on the next page

Aunt	....	....
Father	....	....
Mother	....	....
Uncle	....	....
Brother	....	....
Sister	....	....
Son	....	....
Daughter	....	....
Grandfather	....	....
Sister	....	....
Aunt	....	....
Grandmother	....	....
Uncle	....	....
Son	....	....
Grandmother	....	....
Father	....	....
Brother	....	....
Daughter	....	....
Grandfather	....	....
Mother	....	....

Week 1

Day 4: Food

Bread	Brød [brœd]
Rice	Ris [rees]
Meat	Kjøtt [chyut]
Vegetables	Grønnsaker [GRUN-sah-ker]
Fruit	Frukt [frukt]
Milk	Melk [melk]
Cheese	Ost [ust]
Eggs	Egg [egg]
Soup	Suppe [SOO-peh]
Dessert	Dessert [deh-SERT]

Write the right words down twice on the next page

Cheese	....	....
Meat	....	....
Dessert	....	....
Vegetables	....	....
Fruit	....	....
Milk	....	....
Vegetables	....	....
Eggs	....	....
Soup	....	....
Dessert	....	....
Bread	....	....
Rice	....	....
Meat	....	....
Fruit	....	....
Milk	....	....
Cheese	....	....
Bread	....	....
Eggs	....	....
Soup	....	....
Rice	....	....

Week 1

Day 5: Animals

Dog	Hund [hoond]
Cat	Katt [kat]
Lion	Løve [LUH-veh]
Sheep	Sau [sow]
Pig	Gris [greess]
Ape	Ape [AH-peh]
Tiger	Tiger [TEE-ger]
Bear	Bjørn [byurn]
Horse	Hest [hest]
Bird	Fugl [foogl]

Write the right words down twice on the next page

Ape	....	....
Cat	....	....
Bird	....	....
Lion	....	....
Sheep	....	....
Pig	....	....
Ape	....	....
Tiger	....	....
Bear	....	....
Horse	....	....
Bird	....	....
Dog	....	....
Cat	....	....
Lion	....	....
Sheep	....	....
Pig	....	....
Horse	....	....
Tiger	....	....
Bear	....	....
Dog	....	....

Week 1

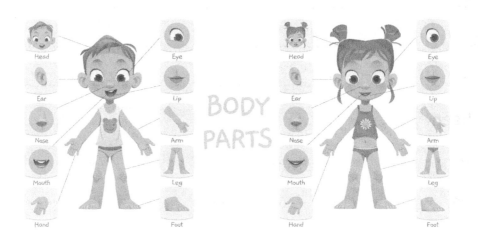

Day 6: Body

Head	Hode [HOO-deh]
Nek	Nakke [nak-keh]
Belly	Mage [MAH-geh]
Shoulder	Skulder [SKOOL-der]
Knee	Kne [kneh]
Back	Rygg [rig]
Arms	Armer [AR-mer]
Hands	Hender [HEN-der]
Legs	Ben [ben]
Feet	Føtter [FUT-ter]

Write the right words down twice on the next page

Shoulder	....	....
Back	....	....
Feet	....	....
Belly	....	....
Hands	....	....
Shoulder	....	....
Knee	....	....
Back	....	....
Arms	....	....
Hands	....	....
Nek	....	....
Feet	....	....
Head	....	....
Nek	....	....
Belly	....	....
Knee	....	....
Legs	....	....
Arms	....	....
Head	....	....
Legs	....	....

Week 1

Day 7: Weather

Sun	Sol [sool]
Rain	Regn [regn]
Cloud	Sky [shee]
Wind	Vind [vind]
Snow	Snø [snuh]
Thunder	Torden [TOR-den]
Lightning	Lyn [leen]
Storm	Storm [storm]
Fog	Tåke [TAW-keh]
Rainbow	Regnbue [REGN-bweh]

Write the right words down twice on the next page

Storm	....	....
Rain	....	....
Fog	....	....
Snow	....	....
Cloud	....	....
Wind	....	....
Snow	....	....
Thunder	....	....
Rain	....	....
Lightning	....	....
Storm	....	....
Fog	....	....
Rainbow	....	....
Sun	....	....
Cloud	....	....
Wind	....	....
Thunder	....	....
Lightning	....	....
Rainbow	....	....
Sun	....	....

Week 2

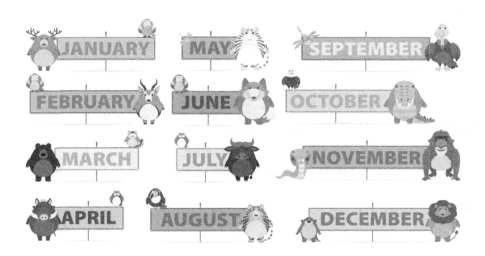

Day 8: Months

January	Januar [yan-WAR]
February	Februar [feh-broo-AR]
May	Mars [mars]
June	April [ah-PREEL]
July	Mai [my]
August	Juni [YOO-nee]
September	Juli [YOO-lee]
October	August [ow-GUST]
November	September [seh-TEM-ber]
December	Oktober [ok-TO-ber]

Write the right words down twice on the next page

October ....

February ....

August ....

October ....

April ....

May ....

June ....

August ....

March ....

September ....

May ....

January ....

July ....

March ....

April ....

June ....

January ....

July ....

February ....

September ....

Week 2

Day 9: School

Teacher	Lærer [LEH-rer]
Student	Student [STOO-dent]
Classroom	Klasserom [KLASS-e-rom]
Book	Bok [book]
Pen	Penn [pen]
Pencil	Blyant [BLY-ant]
Desk	Pult [pult]
Chair	Stol [stool]
Homework	Lekser [LEKS-er]
Exam	Eksamen [eks-AH-men]

Write the right words down twice on the next page

Chair	....	....
Homework	....	....
Teacher	....	....
Student	....	....
Classroom	....	....
Exam	....	....
Pen	....	....
Pencil	....	....
Desk	....	....
Classroom	....	....
Homework	....	....
Exam	....	....
Teacher	....	....
Student	....	....
Desk	....	....
Book	....	....
Pen	....	....
Pencil	....	....
Chair	....	....
Book	....	....

Week 2

Day 10: Transportation

Car	Bil [beel]
Bus	Buss [booss]
Train	Tog [toog]
Bicycle	Sykkel [SIK-kel]
Motorcycle	Motorsykkel [motor-SIK-kel]
Boat	Båt [boat]
Airplane	Fly [flee]
Helicopter	Helikopter [HE-lik-op-ter]
Truck	Lastebil [LAS-te-beel]
Metro	T-bane [TEH-bah-neh]

Write the right words down twice on the next page

Airplane	....	....
Bus	....	....
Train	....	....
Metro	....	....
Truck	....	....
Motorcycle	....	....
Boat	....	....
Airplane	....	....
Helicopter	....	....
Truck	....	....
Metro	....	....
Car	....	....
Bus	....	....
Train	....	....
Bicycle	....	....
Helicopter	....	....
Motorcycle	....	....
Boat	....	....
Bicycle	....	....
Car	....	....

Week 2

Day 11: Clothing

Shirt	Skjorte [shor-teh]
Pants	Bukser [book-ser]
Dress	Kjole [choo-leh]
Skirt	Skjørt [shurt]
Jacket	Jakke [yah-keh]
Shoes	Sko [skoo]
Socks	Sokker [soh-ker]
Hat	Hatt [hat]
Gloves	Hansker [hans-ker]
Scarf	Skjerf [shairf]

Write the right words down twice on the next page

Socks	....	....
Pants	....	....
Dress	....	....
Jacket	....	....
Skirt	....	....
Scarf	....	....
Shoes	....	....
Socks	....	....
Hat	....	....
Gloves	....	....
Scarf	....	....
Shirt	....	....
Pants	....	....
Dress	....	....
Skirt	....	....
Jacket	....	....
Shoes	....	....
Gloves	....	....
Hat	....	....
Shirt	....	....

Week 2

Day 12: Emotions

Happy	Glad [glaad]
Sad	Trist [trist]
Angry	Sint [sint]
Excited	Spent [spent]
Surprised	Overrasket [oo-ver-ra-sket]
Scared	Redd [red]
Nervous	Nervøs [ner-voos]
Bored	Kjedelig [cheh-deh-lig]
Confused	Forvirret [for-vir-ret]
Calm	Rolig [roo-lig]

Write the right words down twice on the next page

Confused ....

Happy ....

Calm ....

Surprised ....

Sad ....

Angry ....

Excited ....

Nervous ....

Scared ....

Nervous ....

Bored ....

Scared ....

Calm ....

Happy ....

Sad ....

Bored ....

Angry ....

Excited ....

Surprised ....

Confused ....

Week 2

Day 13: Hobbies

Reading	Lesing [lee-sing]
Painting	Maling [mah-ling]
Singing	Sang [sahng]
Dancing	Dans [dahns]
Cooking	Matlaging [maht-lah-ging]
Photography	Fotografering [foo-to-gra-feh-ring]
Sleeping	Søvn [suvn]
Writing	Skriving [skree-ving]
Gardening	Hagearbeid [hah-geh-ar-baid]
Sports	Sport [sport]

Write the right words down twice on the next page

Gardening	....	....
Painting	....	....
Photography	....	....
Painting	....	....
Dancing	....	....
Cooking	....	....
Photography	....	....
Sports	....	....
Writing	....	....
Gardening	....	....
Sports	....	....
Reading	....	....
Sleeping	....	....
Singing	....	....
Dancing	....	....
Cooking	....	....
Singing	....	....
Sleeping	....	....
Writing	....	....
Reading	....	....

Week 2

Day 14: Sports

Football	Fotball [fot-ball]
Basketball	Basketball [bas-ket-ball]
Tennis	Tennis [teh-niss]
Swimming	Svømming [svoo-ming]
Volleyball	Volleyball [vol-ley-ball]
Golf	Golf [golf]
Cycling	Sykling [see-kling]
Running	Løping [lur-ping]
Fitness	Fitness [fit-ness]
Martial arts	Kampsport [kamp-sport]

Write the right words down twice on the next page

Swimming	....	....
Football	....	....
Fitness	....	....
Basketball	....	....
Golf	....	....
Swimming	....	....
Volleyball	....	....
Golf	....	....
Running	....	....
Cycling	....	....
Running	....	....
Fitness	....	....
Martial arts	....	....
Football	....	....
Basketball	....	....
Tennis	....	....
Martial arts	....	....
Volleyball	....	....
Cycling	....	....
Tennis	....	....

Week 3

Day 15: Nature

Tree	Tre [treh]
Flower	Blomst [blomst]
River	Elv [elv]
Mountain	Fjell [fyell]
Lake	Sjø [shoo]
Beach	Strand [strahnd]
Forest	Skog [skog]
Grass	Gress [gress]
Star	Stjerne [st-yer-neh]
Cloud	Sky [shee]

Write the right words down twice on the next page

Grass	....	....
Beach	....	....
Mountain	....	....
Cloud	....	....
Flower	....	....
River	....	....
Mountain	....	....
Lake	....	....
Beach	....	....
Forest	....	....
Grass	....	....
Star	....	....
Forest	....	....
Cloud	....	....
Tree	....	....
Flower	....	....
River	....	....
Star	....	....
Lake	....	....
Tree	....	....

Week 3

Day 16: Days of the Week

Monday	Mandag [man-dahg]
Tuesday	Tirsdag [teerz-dahg]
Wednesday	Onsdag [ons-dahg]
Thursday	Torsdag [torz-dahg]
Friday	Fredag [freh-dahg]
Saturday	Lørdag [lur-dahg]
Sunday	Søndag [sun-dahg]
Yesterday	I går [ee gawr]
Tomorrow	I morgen [ee mor-gen]
Today	I dag [ee dahg]

Write the right words down twice on the next page

Sunday	....	....
Tuesday	....	....
Saturday	....	....
Today	....	....
Wednesday	....	....
Tomorrow	....	....
Friday	....	....
Saturday	....	....
Yesterday	....	....
Tomorrow	....	....
Today	....	....
Monday	....	....
Thursday	....	....
Wednesday	....	....
Thursday	....	....
Friday	....	....
Monday	....	....
Sunday	....	....
Yesterday	....	....
Tuesday	....	....

Week 3

Day 17: Music

Song	Sang [sahng]
Melody	Melodi [meh-lo-dee]
Rhythm	Rytme [rit-meh]
Instrument	Instrument [ins-tru-ment]
Singing	Sang [sahng]
Band	Band [band]
Concert	Konsert [kon-sert]
Piano	Piano [pee-ah-no]
Guitar	Gitar [gee-tar]
Sound	Lyd [leed]

Write the right words down twice on the next page

Concert	....	....
Melody	....	....
Rhythm	....	....
Sound	....	....
Guitar	....	....
Piano	....	....
Instrument	....	....
Singing	....	....
Band	....	....
Piano	....	....
Guitar	....	....
Sound	....	....
Song	....	....
Rhythm	....	....
Instrument	....	....
Singing	....	....
Band	....	....
Concert	....	....
Song	....	....
Melody	....	....

Week 3

Day 18: Jobs

Teacher	Lærer [lehr-er]
Doctor	Lege [leh-geh]
Engineer	Ingeniør [ing-eh-nyur]
Chef	Kokk [kok]
Police officer	Politibetjent [pol-ee-tee-bet-yent]
Firefighter	Brannmann [bran-man]
Nurse	Sykepleier [see-keh-plei-er]
Pilot	Pilot [pee-loht]
Lawyer	Advokat [adv-oh-kaht]
Artist	Kunstner [koonst-ner]

Write the right words down twice on the next page

Lawyer	....	....
Teacher	....	....
Chef	....	....
Doctor	....	....
Engineer	....	....
Chef	....	....
Police officer	....	....
Pilot	....	....
Nurse	....	....
Doctor	....	....
Artist	....	....
Teacher	....	....
Pilot	....	....
Engineer	....	....
Artist	....	....
Police officer	....	....
Firefighter	....	....
Nurse	....	....
Lawyer	....	....
Firefighter	....	....

Week 3

Day 19: Fruits

Apple	Eple [ep-leh]
Banana	Banan [bah-nahn]
Orange	Appelsin [ah-pel-seen]
Strawberry	Jordbær [yor-bahr]
Grapes	Druer [droo-er]
Watermelon	Vannmelon [van-mel-on]
Pineapple	Ananas [ah-na-nahs]
Mango	Mango [mang-go]
Kiwi	Kiwi [kee-vee]
Peach	Fersken [fers-ken]

Write the right words down twice on the next page

Orange	....	....
Apple	....	....
Banana	....	....
Orange	....	....
Mango	....	....
Grapes	....	....
Kiwi	....	....
Pineapple	....	....
Mango	....	....
Peach	....	....
Apple	....	....
Banana	....	....
Strawberry	....	....
Grapes	....	....
Watermelon	....	....
Pineapple	....	....
Kiwi	....	....
Strawberry	....	....
Peach	....	....
Watermelon	....	....

Week 3

Day 20: Vegetables

Carrot	Gulrot [gool-rot]
Tomato	Tomat [too-maht]
Potato	Potet [poh-teht]
Onion	Løk [luhk]
Cucumber	Agurk [ah-gurk]
Broccoli	Brokkoli [brok-ko-lee]
Spinach	Spinat [spin-naht]
Corn	Mais [mice]
Cabbage	Kål [kawl]
Mushroom	Sopp [sop]

Write the right words down twice on the next page

Corn	....	....
Tomato	....	....
Potato	....	....
Mushroom	....	....
Spinach	....	....
Onion	....	....
Broccoli	....	....
Spinach	....	....
Corn	....	....
Tomato	....	....
Mushroom	....	....
Carrot	....	....
Cucumber	....	....
Potato	....	....
Onion	....	....
Cucumber	....	....
Cabbage	....	....
Carrot	....	....
Cabbage	....	....
Broccoli	....	....

Week 3

Day 21: Tools

Hammer	Hammer [ham-mer]
Screwdriver	Skrutrekker [skrut-rek-ker]
Wrench	Nøkkel [nuk-kel]
Pliers	Tang [tahng]
Saw	Sag [sahg]
Drill	Bor [boor]
Tape measure	Målebånd [mawl-eh-bawnd]
Chisel	Meisel [my-sel]
Shovel	Spade [spah-deh]
Paintbrush	Malerkost [mah-ler-kost]

Write the right words down twice on the next page

Shovel ....

Screwdriver ....

Wrench ....

Paintbrush ....

Pliers ....

Drill ....

Chisel ....

Shovel ....

Paintbrush ....

Hammer ....

Screwdriver ....

Pliers ....

Saw ....

Drill ....

Tape measure ....

Hammer ....

Wrench ....

Saw ....

Chisel ....

Tape measure ....

Week 4

Day 22: Kitchen

Plate	Tallerken [tal-er-ken]
Fork	Gaffel [gaf-fel]
Knife	Kniv [kneev]
Spoon	Skje [shyeh]
Cup	Kopp [kop]
Bowl	Bolle [bol-leh]
Pan	Pan [pan]
Pot	Gryte [gru-teh]
Cutting board	Skjærebrett [shaere-brett]
Oven	Ovn [ovn]

Write the right words down twice on the next page

Plate ....

Oven ....

Fork ....

Bowl ....

Knife ....

Spoon ....

Cup ....

Cutting board ....

Knife ....

Fork ....

Bowl ....

Spoon ....

Pan ....

Pot ....

Cutting board ....

Oven ....

Pot ....

Plate ....

Cup ....

Pan ....

Week 4

Day 23: Instruments

Guitar	Gitar [gee-tar]
Piano	Piano [pee-ah-no]
Violin	Fiolin [fee-oh-lin]
Flute	Fløyte [floy-teh]
Trumpet	Trompet [trom-pet]
Drum	Tromme [trom-meh]
Saxophone	Saksofon [saks-oh-fon]
Cello	Cello [chel-lo]
Clarinet	Klarinett [klah-ree-net]
Harp	Harpe [har-peh]

Write the right words down twice on the next page

Flute	....	....
Piano	....	....
Trumpet	....	....
Violin	....	....
Cello	....	....
Trumpet	....	....
Drum	....	....
Saxophone	....	....
Cello	....	....
Clarinet	....	....
Violin	....	....
Saxophone	....	....
Harp	....	....
Guitar	....	....
Drum	....	....
Piano	....	....
Harp	....	....
Flute	....	....
Guitar	....	....
Clarinet	....	....

Week 4

Day 24: Buildings

House	Hus [hoos]
School	Skole [sko-leh]
Hospital	Sykehus [see-keh-hoos]
Library	Bibliotek [bib-lee-oh-tek]
Bank	Bank [bank]
Restaurant	Restaurant [res-tah-rangt]
Hotel	Hotell [hoh-tell]
Museum	Museum [moo-seh-um]
Church	Kirke [kir-keh]
Stadium	Stadion [sta-dee-on]

Write the right words down twice on the next page

Hospital	....	....
House	....	....
Museum	....	....
School	....	....
Stadium	....	....
Hospital	....	....
Church	....	....
Restaurant	....	....
Hotel	....	....
Museum	....	....
Church	....	....
House	....	....
School	....	....
Library	....	....
Bank	....	....
Restaurant	....	....
Hotel	....	....
Library	....	....
Bank	....	....
Stadium	....	....

Week 4

Day 25: Directions

Left	Venstre [ven-streh]
Right	Høyre [hoy-reh]
Straight	Rett fram [rett fram]
Up	Opp [op]
Down	Ned [ned]
North	Nord [nord]
South	Sør [sur]
East	Øst [ust]
West	Vest [vest]
Stop	Stopp [stop]

Write the right words down twice on the next page

Straight	………………………….	………………………….
Left	………………………….	………………………….
South	………………………….	………………………….
Straight	………………………….	………………………….
Up	………………………….	………………………….
Down	………………………….	………………………….
North	………………………….	………………………….
Stop	………………………….	………………………….
East	………………………….	………………………….
Stop	………………………….	………………………….
Left	………………………….	………………………….
Right	………………………….	………………………….
South	………………………….	………………………….
Right	………………………….	………………………….
North	………………………….	………………………….
West	………………………….	………………………….
Up	………………………….	………………………….
Down	………………………….	………………………….
East	………………………….	………………………….
West	………………………….	………………………….

Week 4

Day 26: Bedroom

Bed	Seng [seng]
Pillow	Pute [poo-teh]
Blanket	Teppe [tep-peh]
Wardrobe	Garderobe [gard-er-oh-beh]
Nightstand	Nattbord [naht-bord]
Lamp	Lampe [lamp-eh]
Alarm clock	Vekkerklokke [vek-er-klok-keh]
Dresser	Kommode [kom-mo-deh]
Hanger	Kleshenger [klesh-hang-er]
Mirror	Speil [spile]

Write the right words down twice on the next page

Hanger	....	....
Pillow	....	....
Dresser	....	....
Wardrobe	....	....
Mirror	....	....
Nightstand	....	....
Lamp	....	....
Alarm clock	....	....
Dresser	....	....
Blanket	....	....
Hanger	....	....
Mirror	....	....
Wardrobe	....	....
Nightstand	....	....
Bed	....	....
Blanket	....	....
Lamp	....	....
Bed	....	....
Alarm clock	....	....
Pillow	....	....

Week 4

Day 27: Countries

United States	Forente Stater [for-en-teh stah-ter]
United Kingdom	Storbritannia [stor-brit-an-nee-a]
Canada	Canada [kan-a-da]
Australia	Australia [aust-rah-lee-a]
Germany	Tyskland [tiss-land]
France	Frankrike [frank-ri-keh]
China	Kina [kee-na]
Japan	Japan [yah-pan]
Brazil	Brasil [brah-seel]
India	India [in-dee-a]

Write the right words down twice on the next page

China	....	....
United States	....	....
India	....	....
Canada	....	....
Australia	....	....
Brazil	....	....
China	....	....
Japan	....	....
Brazil	....	....
India	....	....
United States	....	....
Germany	....	....
Canada	....	....
Australia	....	....
Japan	....	....
United Kingdom	....	....
Germany	....	....
France	....	....
United Kingdom	....	....
France	....	....

Week 4

Day 28: Travel

Airport	Flyplass [flee-plahss]
Passport	Pass [pahss]
Ticket	Billett [bi-let]
Suitcase	Koffert [ko-fert]
Hotel	Hotell [hoh-tell]
Sightseeing	Sightseeing [sight-seeing]
Beach	Strand [strahnd]
Adventure	Eventyr [ev-en-tyr]
Map	Kart [kart]
Tourist	Turist [too-rist]

Write the right words down twice on the next page

Airport	....	....
Adventure	....	....
Passport	....	....
Ticket	....	....
Suitcase	....	....
Hotel	....	....
Sightseeing	....	....
Beach	....	....
Adventure	....	....
Map	....	....
Tourist	....	....
Airport	....	....
Passport	....	....
Ticket	....	....
Suitcase	....	....
Hotel	....	....
Sightseeing	....	....
Beach	....	....
Map	....	....
Tourist	....	....

Week 5

Day 29: Health

Doctor	Lege [leh-geh]
Hospital	Sykehus [see-keh-hoos]
Medicine	Medisin [meh-di-sin]
Nurse	Sykepleier [see-keh-plei-er]
Pain	Smerte [smair-teh]
Appointment	Timeavtale [ti-meh-avtah-leh]
Exercise	Trening [treh-ning]
Sleep	Søvn [suvn]
Diet	Kosthold [kost-hold]
Vitamin	Vitamin [vit-ah-min]

Write the right words down twice on the next page

Appointment	....	....
Vitamin	....	....
Hospital	....	....
Medicine	....	....
Nurse	....	....
Pain	....	....
Sleep	....	....
Hospital	....	....
Exercise	....	....
Nurse	....	....
Sleep	....	....
Diet	....	....
Vitamin	....	....
Doctor	....	....
Pain	....	....
Appointment	....	....
Exercise	....	....
Doctor	....	....
Medicine	....	....
Diet	....	....

Week 5

Day 30: Languages

English	Engelsk [eng-elsk]
Spanish	Spansk [span-sk]
French	Fransk [fran-sk]
German	Tysk [tisk]
Dutch	Nederlandsk [nether-lan-dsk]
Frisian	Frisisk [fri-sisk]
Russian	Russisk [rus-isk]
Portuguese	Portugisisk [por-too-gis-isk]
Japanese	Japansk [yah-pan-sk]
Italian	Italiensk [it-al-ee-ensk]

Write the right words down twice on the next page

German ....

Spanish ....

Portuguese ....

French ....

German ....

Frisian ....

Dutch ....

Russian ....

Italian ....

Russian ....

Japanese ....

Frisian ....

English ....

Italian ....

English ....

Spanish ....

French ....

Dutch ....

Portuguese ....

Japanese ....

Week 5

Day 31: Church

Priest	Prest [prest]
Worship	Bønn [bunn]
Prayer	Bønn [bunn] (repeated)
Bible	Bibel [bee-bel]
Sermon	Preken [prek-en]
Choir	Kor [kor]
Altar	Alter [al-ter]
Cross	Kors [kors]
Faith	Tro [tro]
Ceremony	Seremoni [ser-eh-mo-nee]

Write the right words down twice on the next page

Choir ....

Worship ....

Altar ....

Bible ....

Ceremony ....

Faith ....

Sermon ....

Choir ....

Altar ....

Cross ....

Faith ....

Ceremony ....

Cross ....

Priest ....

Worship ....

Prayer ....

Bible ....

Sermon ....

Priest ....

Prayer ....

Week 5

Day 32: Birds

Eagle	Ørn [urn]
Sparrow	Spurv [spur-v]
Owl	Ugle [oo-gleh]
Seagull	Papegøye [pa-peh-goy-eh]
Hummingbird	Kolibri [kol-ee-bri]
Pigeon	Due [doo-eh]
Flamingo	Flamingo [fla-ming-oh]
Swan	Svane [sva-neh]
Peacock	Påfugl [po-foog-l]
Duck	And [and]

Write the right words down twice on the next page

Duck	....	....
Eagle	....	....
Sparrow	....	....
Owl	....	....
Eagle	....	....
Swan	....	....
Sparrow	....	....
Flamingo	....	....
Hummingbird	....	....
Pigeon	....	....
Flamingo	....	....
Owl	....	....
Swan	....	....
Peacock	....	....
Duck	....	....
Seagull	....	....
Hummingbird	....	....
Pigeon	....	....
Seagull	....	....
Peacock	....	....

Week 5

Day 33: Science

Chemistry	Kjemi [shem-ee]
Biology	Biologi [bee-o-lo-gee]
Physics	Fysikk [fis-ikk]
Astronomy	Astronomi [as-tro-no-mee]
Experiment	Eksperiment [eks-pe-ri-ment]
Laboratory	Laboratorium [lab-o-ra-to-ri-um]
Microscope	Mikroskop [mik-ro-skop]
Hypothesis	Hypotese [hy-po-te-seh]
Scientist	Forsker [for-sher]
Discovery	Oppdagelse [op-da-gel-seh]

Write the right words down twice on the next page

Hypothesis	....	....
Biology	....	....
Experiment	....	....
Astronomy	....	....
Physics	....	....
Astronomy	....	....
Microscope	....	....
Scientist	....	....
Laboratory	....	....
Physics	....	....
Microscope	....	....
Hypothesis	....	....
Chemistry	....	....
Scientist	....	....
Discovery	....	....
Chemistry	....	....
Biology	....	....
Laboratory	....	....
Discovery	....	....
Experiment	....	....

Week 5

Day 34: Film

Actor	Skuespiller [skues-pil-ler]
Actress	Skuespillerinne [skues-pil-ler-in-neh]
Director	Regissør [reh-gi-shur]
Script	Manus [ma-noos]
Camera	Kamera [ka-mer-a]
Scene	Scene [seh-ne]
Drama	Drama [dra-ma]
Comedy	Komedie [ko-meh-dee]
Action	Action [ak-shon]
Television	Fjernsyn [fyern-syn]

Write the right words down twice on the next page

Actor	....	....
Camera	....	....
Action	....	....
Director	....	....
Script	....	....
Television	....	....
Camera	....	....
Scene	....	....
Drama	....	....
Comedy	....	....
Action	....	....
Television	....	....
Actor	....	....
Actress	....	....
Director	....	....
Scene	....	....
Actress	....	....
Drama	....	....
Comedy	....	....
Script	....	....

Week 5

Day 35: History

Ancient	Antikk [an-tikk]
Civilization	Sivilisasjon [si-vili-sa-shon]
Emperor	Keiser [kai-ser]
Revolution	Revolution [reh-vo-lu-shon]
War	Krig [kreeg]
Kingdom	Kongerike [kon-ge-ri-keh]
Archaeology	Arkeologi [ar-ke-o-lo-gee]
Renaissance	Renessanse [reh-nes-ans-seh]
Independence	Uavhengighet [oo-av-hen-ge-het]
Event	Hendelse [hen-del-seh]

Write the right words down twice on the next page

Kingdom	....	....
Event	....	....
Archaeology	....	....
Emperor	....	....
Renaissance	....	....
Independence	....	....
Revolution	....	....
War	....	....
Kingdom	....	....
Archaeology	....	....
Renaissance	....	....
Independence	....	....
Event	....	....
Ancient	....	....
Civilization	....	....
Emperor	....	....
Revolution	....	....
War	....	....
Ancient	....	....
Civilization	....	....

Week 6

Day 36: Drinks

Water	Vann [van]
Coffee	Kaffe [kaf-feh]
Tea	Te [teh]
Juice	Juice [yoo-se]
Soda	Brus [broos]
Milk	Melk [melk]
Wine	Vin [vin]
Beer	Øl [uhl]
Cocktail	Cocktail [cock-tail]
Lemonade	Sitronade [si-tro-na-deh]

Write the right words down twice on the next page

Soda	....	....
Cocktail	....	....
Tea	....	....
Juice	....	....
Wine	....	....
Soda	....	....
Milk	....	....
Wine	....	....
Beer	....	....
Cocktail	....	....
Lemonade	....	....
Water	....	....
Coffee	....	....
Water	....	....
Tea	....	....
Lemonade	....	....
Juice	....	....
Milk	....	....
Coffee	....	....
Beer	....	....

Week 6

Day 37: Business

Entrepreneur	Gründer [groon-der]
Company	Selskap [sel-shap]
Marketing	Markedsføring [mark-eds-for-ing]
Sales	Salg [salg]
Product	Produkt [pro-dukt]
Customer	Kunde [kun-deh]
Finance	Finans [fee-nans]
Strategy	Strategi [stra-teh-gee]
Profit	Fortjeneste [for-tyen-est-eh]
Investment	Investering [in-ves-te-ring]

Write the right words down twice on the next page

Strategy	....	....
Company	....	....
Marketing	....	....
Sales	....	....
Product	....	....
Customer	....	....
Finance	....	....
Investment	....	....
Customer	....	....
Profit	....	....
Finance	....	....
Investment	....	....
Entrepreneur	....	....
Company	....	....
Marketing	....	....
Sales	....	....
Product	....	....
Profit	....	....
Entrepreneur	....	....
Strategy	....	....

Week 6

Day 38: Beach

Sand	Sand [sand]
Waves	Bølger [bol-ger]
Sunscreen	Solkrem [sol-krem]
Swim	Svømming [svom-ming]
Seashells	Skjell [shel]
Umbrella	Paraply [pa-ra-ply]
Beach ball	Strandball [stran-ball]
Sunbathing	Solbading [sol-ba-ding]
Surfing	Surfing [surf-ing]
Picnic	Piknik [pick-nick]

Write the right words down twice on the next page

Beach ball	....	....
Sunbathing	....	....
Waves	....	....
Sunscreen	....	....
Picnic	....	....
Swim	....	....
Umbrella	....	....
Beach ball	....	....
Picnic	....	....
Sand	....	....
Sunscreen	....	....
Swim	....	....
Seashells	....	....
Surfing	....	....
Waves	....	....
Umbrella	....	....
Seashells	....	....
Sunbathing	....	....
Surfing	....	....
Sand	....	....

Week 6

Day 39: Hospital

Doctor	Lege [leh-geh]
Nurse	Sykepleier [see-keh-plei-er]
Patient	Pasient [pa-si-ent]
Emergency	Nødsituasjon [nurd-si-twa-shon]
Surgery	Kirurgi [kir-ur-gee]
Appointment	Timeavtale [ti-meh-avtah-leh]
Stethoscope	Stetoskop [stet-o-skop]
Sick	Røntgen [runt-gen]
Medicine	Medisin [meh-di-sin]
Recovery	Gjenoppretting [yen-op-pre-tting]

Write the right words down twice on the next page

Nurse ....

Doctor ....

Appointment ....

Stethoscope ....

Emergency ....

Recovery ....

Nurse ....

Patient ....

Emergency ....

Surgery ....

Appointment ....

Stethoscope ....

Sick ....

Medicine ....

Recovery ....

Doctor ....

Surgery ....

Patient ....

Sick ....

Medicine ....

Week 6

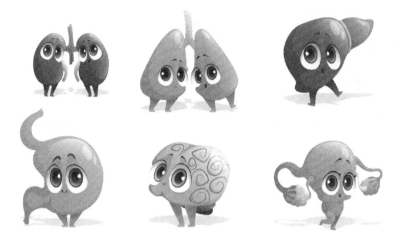

Day 40: Internal Body

Heart	Hjerte [yehr-teh]
Lungs	Lunger [lung-er]
Stomach	Mage [ma-geh]
Liver	Lever [lev-er]
Kidneys	Nyrer [neer-er]
Brain	Hjerne [yehr-neh]
Intestines	Tarm [tarm]
Bladder	Blære [blar-eh]
Bones	Bein [bain]
Muscles	Muskler [mus-kler]

Write the right words down twice on the next page

Kidneys ....

Stomach ....

Heart ....

Intestines ....

Brain ....

Lungs ....

Stomach ....

Liver ....

Muscles ....

Kidneys ....

Intestines ....

Bladder ....

Bones ....

Muscles ....

Heart ....

Lungs ....

Bones ....

Liver ....

Brain ....

Bladder ....

Week 6

Day 41: Internet

Website	Nettsted [net-sted]
Email	E-post [e-post]
Social media	Sosiale medier [so-sia-le me-di-er]
Online shopping	Netthandel [net-hand-el]
Search engine	Søkemotor [suh-ke-mo-tor]
Password	Passord [pass-ord]
Wi-Fi	Wi-Fi [wee-fee]
Download	Nedlasting [ned-last-ing]
Upload	Opplasting [op-last-ing]
Browser	Nettleser [net-le-ser]

Write the right words down twice on the next page

Browser ....

Website ....

Email ....

Social media ....

Wi-Fi ....

Search engine ....

Password ....

Wi-Fi ....

Download ....

Upload ....

Browser ....

Online shopping ....

Email ....

Social media ....

Online shopping ....

Password ....

Website ....

Download ....

Upload ....

Search engine ....

Week 6

Day 42: Shapes

Cirkel	Sirkel [sir-kel]
Square	Firkant [fir-kant]
Rectangle	Rektangel [rek-tan-gel]
Triangle	Trekant [tre-kant]
Oval	Oval [o-val]
Pyramid	Pyramide [pyra-mi-de]
Cube	Kube [koo-be]
Arrow	Pil [peel]
Star	Stjerne [st-yer-neh]
Cylinder	Sylinder [sil-in-der]

Write the right words down twice on the next page

Rectangle	....	....
Triangle	....	....
Pyramid	....	....
Arrow	....	....
Star	....	....
Cylinder	....	....
Oval	....	....
Square	....	....
Star	....	....
Cube	....	....
Cirkel	....	....
Pyramid	....	....
Cylinder	....	....
Cirkel	....	....
Square	....	....
Rectangle	....	....
Triangle	....	....
Oval	....	....
Cube	....	....
Arrow	....	....

Week 7

Day 43: House Parts

Roof	Tak [taak]
Door	Dør [door]
Window	Vindu [vin-du]
Floor	Gulv [goolv]
Wall	Vegg [vegg]
Ceiling	Tak [taak] (Yes, "tak" means both "ceiling" and "roof" in Norwegian)
Stairs	Trapper [tra-paer]
Bathroom	Baderom [baa-deh-room]
Kitchen	Kjøkken [chuh-ken]
Bedroom	Soverom [soo-ve-room]

Write the right words down twice on the next page

Wall	....	....
Door	....	....
Stairs	....	....
Ceiling	....	....
Floor	....	....
Wall	....	....
Ceiling	....	....
Bedroom	....	....
Stairs	....	....
Bathroom	....	....
Kitchen	....	....
Bedroom	....	....
Roof	....	....
Door	....	....
Window	....	....
Floor	....	....
Roof	....	....
Bathroom	....	....
Kitchen	....	....
Window	....	....

Week 7

Day 44: Around the House

Plant	Plante [plan-te]
Watering can	Vannkanne [van-kah-ne]
Shed	Redskapsbod [red-skaps-bod]
Doorbell	Dørklokke [door-klok-keh]
Fence	Gjerde [yehr-deh]
Mailbox	Postkasse [post-kas-seh]
Lawn mower	Gressklipper [gress-klip-per]
Wheelbarrow	Trillebår [tril-le-baar]
Shovel	Spade [spa-deh]
Bench	Benk [benk]

Write the right words down twice on the next page

Watering can	....	....
Shed	....	....
Doorbell	....	....
Mailbox	....	....
Bench	....	....
Fence	....	....
Wheelbarrow	....	....
Shed	....	....
Mailbox	....	....
Bench	....	....
Lawn mower	....	....
Wheelbarrow	....	....
Shovel	....	....
Plant	....	....
Watering can	....	....
Doorbell	....	....
Fence	....	....
Lawn mower	....	....
Shovel	....	....
Plant	....	....

Week 7

Day 45: Face

Eyes	Øyne [øyn-eh]
Nose	Nese [neh-seh]
Mouth	Munn [mun]
Ears	Ører [ø-rer]
Cheeks	Kinn [chin]
Forehead	Panne [pan-neh]
Chin	Hake [haa-keh]
Lips	Lepper [lep-per]
Teeth	Tenner [ten-ner]
Eyebrows	Øyenbryn [ø-yan-bryn]

Write the right words down twice on the next page

Eyebrows	....	....
Nose	....	....
Chin	....	....
Forehead	....	....
Ears	....	....
Cheeks	....	....
Forehead	....	....
Chin	....	....
Nose	....	....
Lips	....	....
Teeth	....	....
Eyebrows	....	....
Eyes	....	....
Lips	....	....
Teeth	....	....
Mouth	....	....
Ears	....	....
Mouth	....	....
Cheeks	....	....
Eyes	....	....

Week 7

Day 46: Bathroom

Sink	Vask [vask]
Toilet	Toalett [too-a-lett]
Shower	Dusj [doosh]
Bathtub	Badekar [ba-deh-kar]
Mirror	Speil [spayl]
Towel	Håndkle [hond-kle]
Soap	Såpe [saa-peh]
Toothbrush	Tannbørste [tan-bør-steh]
Shampoo	Sjampo [sham-po]
Hairdryer	Hårføner [haar-foon-er]

Write the right words down twice on the next page

Mirror	....	....
Sink	....	....
Hairdryer	....	....
Shower	....	....
Bathtub	....	....
Mirror	....	....
Towel	....	....
Soap	....	....
Toothbrush	....	....
Toilet	....	....
Shampoo	....	....
Towel	....	....
Soap	....	....
Hairdryer	....	....
Sink	....	....
Toilet	....	....
Shower	....	....
Bathtub	....	....
Toothbrush	....	....
Shampoo	....	....

Week 7

Day 47: Living Room

Sofa	Sofa [so-fa]
Television	Fjernsyn [fyern-syn]
Coffee table	Salongbord [sa-long-bord]
Bookshelf	Bokhylle [bok-hyl-le]
Lamp	Lampe [lamp-eh]
Rug	Teppe [tep-peh]
Cushion	Puter [poo-ter]
Remote control	Fjernkontroll [fyern-kon-troll]
Curtains	Gardiner [gard-in-er]
Fireplace	Peis [pay-s]

Write the right words down twice on the next page

Rug ....

Sofa ....

Remote control ....

Television ....

Coffee table ....

Bookshelf ....

Lamp ....

Cushion ....

Curtains ....

Fireplace ....

Sofa ....

Television ....

Fireplace ....

Lamp ....

Rug ....

Cushion ....

Remote control ....

Curtains ....

Bookshelf ....

Coffee table ....

Week 7

Day 48: Finance

Budget	Budsjett [bud-shett]
Savings	Sparing [spa-ring]
Debt	Gjeld [yeld]
Income	Inntekt [inn-tekt]
Expenses	Utgifter [oot-gifter]
Bank account	Bankkonto [bank-kon-to]
Credit card	Kredittkort [kre-ditt-kort]
Interest	Rente [ren-teh]
Loan	Lån [loon]
Stock market	Aksjemarked [aks-je-marked]

Write the right words down twice on the next page

Savings	....	....
Loan	....	....
Debt	....	....
Income	....	....
Expenses	....	....
Budget	....	....
Income	....	....
Expenses	....	....
Interest	....	....
Loan	....	....
Stock market	....	....
Budget	....	....
Bank account	....	....
Credit card	....	....
Debt	....	....
Savings	....	....
Interest	....	....
Bank account	....	....
Credit card	....	....
Stock market	....	....

Week 7

Day 49: Books

Writer	Forfatter [for-fatter]
Page	Side [si-deh]
Table of Contents	Innholdsfortegnelse [inn-holds-for-teg-nel-s
Foreword	Forord [for-ord]
Introduction	Introduksjon [intro-duks-jon]
Front cover	Forside [for-si-de]
Back cover	Baksiden [bak-si-den]
Text	Tekst [tekst]
Title	Tittel [tit-tel]
Picture	Bilde [bil-deh]

Write the right words down twice on the next page

Front cover ....

Table of Contents ....

Title ....

Picture ....

Introduction ....

Back cover ....

Page ....

Foreword ....

Title ....

Text ....

Back cover ....

Picture ....

Writer ....

Page ....

Table of Contents ....

Foreword ....

Introduction ....

Front cover ....

Writer ....

Text ....

Week 8

Day 50: Law

Witness	Vitne [vit-neh]
Justice	Rettferdighet [rett-fer-dig-het]
Judge	Dommer [dom-mer]
Victim	Offer [off-er]
Perpetrator	Gjerningsmann [yern-ings-man]
Court	Domstol [dom-stol]
Evidence	Bevis [be-vis]
Lawyer	Advokat [ad-vo-kat]
Crime	Kriminalitet [krim-i-na-li-tet]
Government	Regjering [reg-yer-ing]

Write the right words down twice on the next page

Perpetrator	....	....
Court	....	....
Justice	....	....
Evidence	....	....
Victim	....	....
Government	....	....
Judge	....	....
Victim	....	....
Perpetrator	....	....
Court	....	....
Evidence	....	....
Lawyer	....	....
Crime	....	....
Government	....	....
Witness	....	....
Justice	....	....
Crime	....	....
Judge	....	....
Witness	....	....
Lawyer	....	....

Help Us Share Your Thoughts!

Dear Reader,

Thank you for choosing to read our book. We hope you enjoyed the journey through its pages and that it left a positive impact on your life. As an independent author, reviews from readers like you are incredibly valuable in helping us reach a wider audience and improve our craft.

If you enjoyed our book, we kindly ask for a moment of your time to leave an honest review. Your feedback can make a world of difference by providing potential readers with insight into the book's content and your personal experience.

Your review doesn't have to be lengthy or complicated—just a few lines expressing your genuine thoughts would be immensely appreciated. We value your feedback and take it to heart, using it to shape our future work and create more content that resonates with readers like you.

By leaving a review, you are not only supporting us as authors but also helping other readers discover this book. Your voice matters, and your words have the power to inspire others to embark on this literary journey.

We genuinely appreciate your time and willingness to share your thoughts. Thank you for being an essential part of our author journey.

Made in the USA
Monee, IL
28 December 2023

50720896R10059